Practices for Overcoming Anxiety

More than 40 practices

- Understand your anxiety
- Act on your anxiety

Boussaidane S, M.D.

THIS WORKBOOK BELONGS TO

CONTENTS

Introduction   vi

How to use this book   viii

Part 1 – Understand your anxiety

Note the stimulus that generates anxiety   2

The thoughts and ideas that are generated   4

Manifestation of anxiety   6

Interpretations of symptoms   12

Part 2 – Act on your anxiety

Focus on the things that worry you   16

Challenge your thought pattern   18

Confronting fears   20

Practice deep breathing   22

Practice progressive muscle relaxation   24

Practice meditation   26

Have a balanced diet   28

Certain dietary changes can help   30

Prevent hypoglycemia   32

Drink enough water   34

Are you drinking too much coffee?   36

Are you drinking alcohol?   38

Certain medications can cause or worsen anxiety   40

Plan meals   42

Do physical activity   44

Get enough sleep   46

Take a nap   48

Do you wake up late?   50

Are you often late?   52

Check to see if your job is a source of anxiety   54

Avoid traffic jams   56

Take a hot bath   58

Use aromatherapy   60

You live in messy?   62

Avoid the noise   64

Do you suffer from the past?   66

Are you worried about the future?   68

Are you stressed due to financial issues?   70

Do you find yourself in annoying discussions?   72

Make others happy   74

Be careful of social media   76

Do you spend too much time alone?   80

Don't hesitate to ask for help   84

Walk in nature   86

Learn to say "no"   88

Learn to say "yes"   90

Do hobbies   92

Spend quality time with your family   94

Laugh more   96

Laugh at yourself   98

Make a to-do list   100

Take the agenda   102

INTRODUCTION

Anxiety is an emotion characterized by feelings of tension, worried thoughts and physical changes like increased blood pressure. It corresponds to the more or less conscious expectation of a danger or a problem to come. Anxiety is a normal phenomenon, present in all individuals: fear before an exam, facing a difficult problem at work, worrying about a parent's health, anxious reactions during accidents, etc. Anxiety can give you a boost of energy, help you focus and cope. However, it can take on an excessive and chronic character and become disabling on a daily basis, we will then speak of anxiety disorders.

Anxiety manifests itself in psychological symptoms (fear, anguish, nervousness, fatigue, difficulty concentrating, irritability) and sometimes distressing physical symptoms: heart palpitations, muscle tension, headaches or stomach aches, diarrhea or constipation, feeling of suffocation, sweating, hot or cold flashes, feeling of a lump in the throat or stomach, insomnia, etc. The physical symptoms do not always suggest anxiety and the patient is worried about having another disease.

The treatment of anxiety is based on psychotherapy, possibly in combination with medication if the symptoms are too difficult to bear. Once you've been diagnosed with anxiety, you can explore treatment options with your doctor. For some patients, medical treatment is not necessary and lifestyle changes may be enough to cope with anxiety. There are many things you can do on your own to help reduce your anxiety, such as: relaxation, meditation, regular exercise, etc.

SCHEMA OF ANXIETY

The process of genesis of certain anxiety disorders, the appearance of an anxiety attack and its evolution can be explained by the focus and the interpretation that are made by the patient.

From an external or internal stimulus generating anxiety, the person can have an automatic thought that is a source of more or less intense worry which will be expressed in different ways and the patient can have psychological symptoms and physical symptoms. Little by little or very quickly depending on the case, the person will focus more and more on his physical symptoms and/or on psychic events.

The evolution will depend on the interpretation that he will make of it. Either it turns out to be positive, reassuring and his level of anxiety will tend not to increase, if not to subside and possibly even to disappear completely. Either the interpretation of the symptoms is negative, which will be responsible for their strengthening, which can lead to a real anxiety attack. The regular repetition of this functioning for a period of time can lead to the onset of an anxiety disorder which will manifest itself in significant suffering.

Self-confidence influences the relationship between the intensity of anxiety and the interpretation of symptoms. In cases of high self-confidence, the increase in symptoms leads to positive perceptions of control and facilitative interpretations.

HOW TO USE THIS BOOK

This book helps you adopt tips and strategies for better managing stress and anxiety.

The first part will allow you to identify the triggers, symptoms and interpretations, in order to better understand and decipher your anxiety in order to cut its circle.

The second part contains self-help strategies to act on your anxiety, such as changing the way of thinking, doing exercises, changing bad habits and living healthily.

Each time a focused topic you will be working on. There you'll find explanations of why you should work on it, practical tips, and a place to interact, rate, and express yourself.

Keep this book with you which could quickly become your best friend. Reuse it whenever necessary.

UNDERSTAND YOUR ANXIETY

Note the external stimulus that generates anxiety: changes in working conditions, environment, events, circumstances, situation, obligations, and so on.

Or

internal stimulus that generates anxiety: physical state (hormonal changes, illness or fear of being ill), thoughts (feelings of anger and anxiety) and behaviors (the way you eat and sleep).

The thoughts and ideas that are generated as a result of this anxiety.
"The arrival of a small negative inner voice"

i don't know how to do, i can't do, even if i do it will be bad, i was not ready for this, i'm not going to be up to it...

MANIFESTATION OF ANXIETY

PSYCHIC SYMPTOMS

○ Fear

○ Nervousness

○ Irritability

○ Difficulty concentrating

○ Distraction

○ Anguish

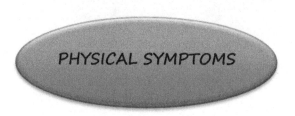

PHYSICAL SYMPTOMS

○ Sleeping troubles

○ Dizziness

○ Headache

○ Feeling of tightness in the chest

○ Heart palpitations

○ Tremors

○ Sweaty hands

○ Hot or cold flashes

○ Chills

○ Muscle aches

○ Nausea

○ Stomach aches

○ Diarrhea or Constipation

○ Frequent urination

⭕ **Others**

Note your interpretations either negative or positive of the symptoms.

ACT ON YOUR ANXIETY

Self-Help Strategies for Anxiety

Focus objectively on the things that worry you to decrease anxiety levels. Classify your fears, for example "if you lose your job". Then assess the likelihood of it happening based on a score of 1 to 10, with 1 being the least likely score and 10 being the most likely score. You will be surprised to find that there are few responses with a score greater than 5. If one response scores greater than 5, you can make a contingency plan for that situation. Having a plan of action that promises positive results helps you reduce your anxiety.

FEARS	SCORE

FEARS	SCORE

Challenge your thought pattern. Negative thoughts can take hold of your mind and distort the gravity of the situation. Make a complete break with systematic negative thinking and immediately change your mind about the anxiety-inducing cause you have identified. This strategy consists of replacing "anxious" or "worried" thinking with realistic and balanced thinking.

Confronting Fears: An important strategy for dealing with anxiety is dealing with situations, places or objects that make you anxious. It's okay to want to avoid the things you fear. The process of facing fears is called EXPOSURE. He is not dangerous and will not increase fear, if done the right way. Starting with less frightening situations, you work your way up to dealing with things that causes you a lot of anxiety. Try to make a list of feared situations, places or objects, classify them from the least frightening to the most frightening.

Practice deep breathing. You tend to breathe faster when you are anxious, so the deep breathing strategy is used to calm your anxiety and help you take back control of your well-being.

To practice deep breathing:

• Try this exercise whenever you need to relax anytime, anywhere.

• Sit or lie flat in a comfortable position.

• Put one hand on your belly and the other hand on your chest.

• Breathe in deeply through your nose enough so that the hand on your abdomen goes up and the one on your chest barely moves.

• Hold the air in your lungs, and Breathe out through pursed lips as if you are blowing through a straw. Feel the hand on your belly go in.

• Repeat this cycle 3 to 10 times. Take your time with each breath.

• Take a moment to notice how you feel at the end of this breathing exercise.

Notice the effectiveness of the deep breathing exercise in terms of improving your daily well-being.

Practice progressive muscle relaxation. It teaches you to relax your body. Tightening and relaxing the muscles throughout your body can help reduce your overall tension and stress levels, teach you what relaxation feels like and how you recognize stress when it starts.

Advice for good practices:

•You don't need to be anxious when doing this exercise. In fact, it' best to start when you're calm. This way it will be easier to d when you are feeling anxious.

•Find a calm place where you can perform this exercis undisturbed.

•**Tension**: For each muscle group (body area) listed below, you appl muscle tension. First, focus on the target muscle group, fo example your left foot. Then, breathe slowly and deeply and tighte the muscles as loud as possible for about 5 seconds (Be careful Yo should never feel severe or throbbing pain while performing thi exercise).

•**Relaxing**: Let all the tension escape from the tight muscles. Exhal as you do this step. notice how the feeling of relaxation i different from feeling tense.

•Stay in this state for about 15 seconds, then move on to the nex muscle group. After you have completed all the muscle groups, tak some time to enjoy the state of relaxation.

MUSCLE GROUPS
•**Foot** (Curl your toes down)
•**Calves** (Point or flex your feet)
•**Thighs** (Clench them hard)
•**Hands** (Clench fist)
•**Arms** (Make fists and squeeze them toward your shoulders)
   (Repeat on other side of body)
•**Buttocks** (Tighten by bringing your buttocks together)
•**Belly** (Suck the belly)
•**Chest** (Tighten by taking a deep breath)
•**Shoulders** (Raise your shoulders up to touch your ears)
•**Face** (Scrunch your facial features to the center of your face)
•**Whole body** (Squeeze all muscles together)

How helpful have you found the practice of progressive muscle relaxation in managing anxiety? Notice your experience.

Learn to meditate and do it regularly to calm yourself down and relax. Meditation is the practice of training the mind to free itself from negative and harmful thoughts. Obviously, there are many thoughts that are helpful in managing your life. But, the thoughts that constantly arise and invade you are often deleterious. The goal of meditation is therefore to free you from your negative ruminations which control you and prevent you from moving forward in your life.

Mindfulness meditation. It is a type of meditation that is based on awareness and acceptance of living in the present moment.

Tips and examples for practicing mindfulness:

•You can do the mindfulness exercises anywhere and anytime.

•Discover your surroundings with all your senses (sight, touch, hearing, smell and taste). For example, when you eat a food, take the time to smell it, to taste it without judgment or when you walk, feel the air pass in front of the body and always without judgment.

•Pay attention to the breathing sensations on exhalation and inhalation.

•Pay attention to the parts of the body. Focus your attention slowly and deliberately on each part of your body, in order, from toe to head or from head to toe.

•Bring your attention back whenever the mind begins to wander.

•Make your daily tasks an opportunity to meditate.

•Whenever you do a mindfulness practice, tell yourself that the most important thing is to be present. Catch your breath and observe without judgment.

Describe your experience practicing mindfulness and your success in being in the present moment.

Are you sure your diet is balanced? It has been observed that eating a balanced diet rich in beneficial nutrients is associated with improved mental health.

For a healthy diet:

•Diversified the diet by eating different types of foods and changing the amounts and types of substances including fruits, vegetables, legumes, nuts and whole grains.

•Eat vegetables and fruit daily, at least 400g (or 5 servings of 80-100g each) per day. It is preferable to eat fresh fruits and vegetables that are in season.

•Substances that contain fat are also beneficial to the body, but it is recommended that the total fat intake is less than 30% of the daily energy intake. And it is recommended to eat unsaturated fats, such as avocados, olive oil, peanut butter, peanut oil, vegetable oils, fatty fish, nuts and seeds.

•Less than 10% of total energy intake from free sugars, which is equivalent to 50 grams (or about 12 level teaspoons) for a person of healthy body weight consuming about 2,000 calories per day. Free sugars are all sugars added to foods or drinks by the manufacturer, cook or consumer, as well as sugars naturally found in honey, syrup, fruit juices, and fruit juice concentrates. Sugar intake can be reduced by eating fresh fruits and raw vegetables as snacks instead of sugary snacks.

•Limit salt to less than 5 grams of salt (equivalent to about 1 teaspoon) per day. The salt should be iodized.

Write down the eating habits you want to stop.

Certain dietary changes can help balance mood and better manage symptoms of anxiety. Before trying the changes make sure you're getting enough fruits, vegetables, protein, whole carbohydrates, and healthy fats. Then, you can introduce and observe the effects of these foods listed below on your mood.

•**Oily fish**, such as salmon, mackerel, sardines, trout, and herring are rich in omega-3s, which play an essential role in brain function and its nutritional deficiency produces the behavioral and neurobiological effects of stress.

•**Dark chocolate** helps drastically reduce stress. Make sure you choose dark chocolate which contains 90% cocoa to really see the effects.

•**Seeds and nuts** by the substances they contain can help you fight anxiety effectively.

•**Leafy greens** like kale and spinach help produce the beneficial chemicals "dopamine and serotonin".

•**Citrus fruits** are excellent sources of vitamin C which help balance the body biochemically and physiologically and cope with stress especially in times of stress our body needs more vitamin C.

•Including **yogurt**, other **dairy products**, and **fermented foods** in the diet can benefit natural gut bacteria and can reduce anxiety and stress.

•**Green tea** contains an amino acid called theanine, which has anxiolytic and calming effects and is also a suitable substitute for soft drinks, coffee, and alcoholic beverages. You can consume **chamomile** tea thanks to the relaxing and anxiolytic properties of the flavonoids present in chamomile.

•**Eggs** contain tryptophan, an amino acid that helps create serotonin a chemical neurotransmitter that helps regulate mood, sleep, memory, improves brain function, and relieves anxiety.

•**Turmeric** contains the active substance, curcumin, which is known to reduce anxiety and works particularly on inflammation and oxidative stress, which increase in people with mood disorders such as anxiety and depression.

What is the place of these substances on your plate?

Are you hypoglycaemic? When your blood sugar drops, your body tries to raise it by secreting adrenaline. If it stays there, your body makes more hormones, including cortisol. Put adrenaline and cortisol (stress hormones) together and you have a recipe for anxiety. When you are stressed you often have a lack of appetite and if you skip meals you will have hypoglycemia (low blood sugar levels), which fuels your anxiety. It's a vicious circle.

Preventive measures:

• To eat your meals at fixed times and not to skip them.

• The food must provide enough energy. But you should avoid simple sugars (refined sugar, powdered or lump sugar, caramel, sweets, sodas, etc). Instead, opt for complex carbohydrates like those in whole grains, vegetables, fruits and legumes provide fiber. It is recommended that carbohydrates make up 45 to 65 percent of your total daily calories. So if you are consuming 2,000 calories per day, between 900 and 1,300 calories should come from carbohydrates. This translates to between 225 and 325 grams of carbohydrate per day. You can find the carbohydrate content of packaged foods on the Nutrition Facts label.

• Exercise regularly, but in moderation, avoiding strenuous and intense exercise.

Write down your action plan for healthy eating.

Are you drinking enough water? According to many studies, there is a link between dehydration and the increased risk of having anxiety. The benefits of water on the brain are multiple. Water goes into the production of neurotransmitters like serotonin. Even moderate dehydration decreases alertness, increases feelings of fatigue, and increases anxiety levels.

Tips for drinking more water:

•You can set reminders to drink water using an app or the alarm on your smartphone or smartwatch.

•The more you love your water bottle, the more likely you are to use it every day. Opt for a stainless steel water bottle, with patterns that appeal to you.

•Use a straw for your water consumption. With a reusable stainless steel or bamboo straw, you drink more, and faster. You'll be well hydrated before you even know it.

•Keeping the bottle with you throughout the day can help you drink more water.

•Refill as soon as the bottle is empty.

•Drink before you are thirsty. When it is felt, the body has already lost too much water.

•Increase consumption in the event of heat, fever or exercise.

•Make each of the transitions (getting out of bed, going to bed, brushing your teeth, eating, doing the dishes, going for a walk, etc.) by drinking water.

•If you want to vary the taste, try incorporating different flavors into your water. Lemon, oranges, mint, strawberries, basil, lavender, etc.

•Eat foods high in water such as cucumber, lettuce, radish, watermelon, cantaloupe, honeydew melon, tomato, spinach, broccoli, peppers, strawberries, and other raw fruits and vegetables, can contribute to your daily intake of water.

Are you drinking too much coffee? In high doses, caffeine can wake up your anxiety and affect your sleep. Lack of sleep, in turn, can make you anxious.

▪Watch out for the harmful effects of caffeine:

•It stimulates the production of the stress hormones "cortisol and adrenaline", which triggers anxiety.

•It depletes your reserves of minerals (like magnesium) that allow you to fight anxiety.

▪Some advices:

•Some anxious patients can drink coffee, but in moderation (one cup of coffee per day). You need to watch how much caffeine you swallow each day. Beware of substances that contain caffeine without realizing it (tea, chocolate, guarana, certain flavorings, certain soft drinks, certain drugs...).

•There are precautions you can take to reduce the effects of caffeine: drink enough water, get caffeine as soon as possible, get moving and make sure you eat a balanced diet that will prevent you from any magnesium deficiency.

Monitor your physical symptoms of anxiety to determine if the level of caffeine you are consuming is too high.

Many people report drinking to reduce anxiety or stress. Alcohol intake may become more regular, resulting in chronic alcohol consumption which induces anxiety disorder. Yet epidemiological studies show that alcohol neither protects nor cures anxiety disorders. On the other hand, alcohol would even be an inducer of anxiety disorder.

Stopping alcohol alone will help avoid worsening your mental and physical situation. For alcohol withdrawal, it is possible to consult an addictologist or a psychiatrist for psychological support possibly combined with medication.

Note the current level of consumption (number of drinks per day).

▪Meds Might Cause Anxiety:

Medications With Caffeine: Acetaminophen and caffeine; Aspirin and caffeine; Ergotamine and caffeine.

ADHD Drugs: Amphetamine; Dextroamphetamine; Dexmethylphenidate; Lisdexamfetamine; Methylphenidate.

Corticosteroids: Cortisone; Dexamethasone; Prednisone.

Decongestants: Pseudoephedrine; Phenylephrine.

Antihistamines: Diphenhydramine; Loratadine; Cetirizine; Fexofenadine; Levocetirizine.

Rescue inhalers: Albuterol; Salmeterol.

Seizure Drugs: Phenytoin.

Medicine for Parkinson's Disease: Levodopa; Carbidopa.

Thyroid Medicine: Levothyroxine; Liothyronine.

Tapering medications: Sometimes it is not the medication that causes the anxiety, but the lack of it. Medications like stimulants, antidepressants, anxiolytics can cause rebound anxiety if they are stopped suddenly or if you reduce them too quickly.

•If you think the anxiety might be from a medication, or if you notice changes in mood or behavior after you start taking a medication. Talk to your doctor, he may adjust your dose or switch you to another medicine.

•If you are taking any medications, watch them.

MEDICATION

Medication	Dose	Frequency	Notes

Plan meals in advance to reduce the stress and pressure associated with meal preparation. You start prep after feeling hungry or pressed for time. The tension builds you open the refrigerator and suddenly you fee overwhelmed and stressed. Set aside a time in the week to make a meal plan for the week will pay you big benefit later in the week. You will feel more energetic, focused and productive.

How to successfully plan meals?

•You list the foods already in the refrigerator, freezer and pantry Complete with products that you want to put on the menu.

•Consider the menu for the week when choosing foods for a fu meal. First cook the foods you already have in the refrigerator.

•At the beginning, you don't have to plan all the meals for the week Start with one meal, then two, and so on. You can also only schedul suppers.

•When planning, also take a look at the schedule: work, outing: leisure, family time ... If the schedule is too busy, prepare a dis that requires little preparation.

•Write a list of foods to buy. You are now ready to go grocer shopping.

•You can implement this practice at a time that is convenient fo you but preferably on weekends, for example by starting plannin on Friday, doing groceries on Saturday, then using about an hour o Sunday for meal preparation.

•Meal planning should be flexible, with so much room fc experimentation, quick reviews, and personalization.

Write a plan for successful meal planning.

Among the best tips for stress and anxiety, exercise. Many studies show that exercise is associated with reduced anxiety. Physical activity helps release endorphins and also breaks the cycle of negative thoughts that fuel anxiety. They provide a feeling of well-being and help the body to relax.

What is the recommended amount of physical activity for an adult?

•Adults should spend at least 150-300 minutes per week in moderate-intensity aerobic physical activity.

•Or at least 75 to 150 minutes of vigorous-intensity aerobic physical activity; or an equivalent combination of moderate and vigorous-intensity activity throughout the week.

•Add moderate to high intensity muscle-strengthening activities (such as resistance or weights) involving major muscle groups at least 2 days per week, as these provide additional health benefits.

•May increase moderate-intensity aerobic physical activity to more than 300 minutes; or do more than 150 minutes of vigorous-intensity aerobic physical activity; or an equivalent combination of moderate- and vigorous-intensity activity throughout the week for additional benefits.

•Should limit sedentary time. Replace a sedentary lifestyle with physical activity of any intensity (including light: slow walking, watering the garden, etc.), interrupting prolonged periods spent in a sitting or lying position, at least every 90 to 120 minutes, through physical activity such as walking for a few minutes.

Current physical activity

Type of physical activity	Frequency	Intensity	Duration per session

Physical activity goal

Type of physical activity	Frequency	Intensity	Duration per session

Are you not getting enough sleep? Lack of sleep causes anxiety, and anxiety can cause insomnia, it's a vicious cycle. In addition, if insomnia becomes chronic, it can increase the risk of depression and anxiety disorders. Good sleep habits can help you get a good night's sleep which is important for physical and mental health, and positively affects productivity and overall quality of life.

Some habits that can improve your sleep health:

•Identify your need for sleep. Each individual has their own need for sleep. Some people said they will need less than 6 hours per night, others will struggle with 7 hours. The ideal is therefore to identify your needs by keeping an updated sleep diary for a month in which will be recorded the time of bedtime, waking up, the duration of sleep and the feeling of tiredness or drowsiness during the daytime.

•Go to bed at the first signs of fatigue such as yawning, tingling in the eyes, difficulty concentrating that the body sends indicating that it is ready to fall asleep. If ignored, it takes at least 90 minutes (the length of a sleep cycle) for the urge to sleep to return.

•Maintain as much regularity as possible in your hours of sleep.

•Avoid stimulants after 4 p.m. such as coffee, chocolate, soft drinks and any other stimulating substance.

•Avoid sport two hours before bedtime. However physical exercise during the day promotes falling asleep and sleep.

•In the evening, don't eat too early or too late. Plan to eat at least two hours before going to bed. Avoid heavy meals, rich in fats and sugars. Likewise, the feeling of hunger disrupts sleep. The ideal is therefore to make a dinner that is neither too light nor too filling.

•Create an environment to sleep well. A room with dim lights and a soft atmosphere with an ambient temperature between 60 and 67°F (15.6 and 19.4°C) will help you fall asleep quickly.

Note your bad sleeping habits.

Your behavior for a good sleep.

Take a nap to take a step back. A quick nap in the middle of the day can do wonders for your health, whether it boosts your memory or lowers your blood pressure, or when you don't sleep well, it can help you recover. Naps are also helpful in regulating emotions and relieving anxiety. In short, after a nap, things get better.

Some tips for taking a nap:

•Make sure you have a dark room or an eye mask for less light.

•Try to plan your nap for earlier in the day. You can schedule the nap at the end of the morning or at the beginning of the afternoon (before 3 p.m.).

•Set your bedroom temperature to a comfortable level before your nap.

•Find a comfortable and quiet place that suits your lifestyle and where you are (your bed, your office, your sofa, etc). It is better to lie down so as not to sleep in an uncomfortable position.

•It's better if the nap is short. It usually lasts ten to twenty minutes. Beyond that, you break the cycle when it is more advanced and your brain has entered a phase of deep sleep, you wake up totally disoriented and this can disrupt the biological clock and have a negative impact on your nighttime sleep which is the most restorative. So make sure you have an alarm clock set for about 2 minutes to reap the benefits of your nap.

What is the place of the nap in your life? Note its effects.

Do you wake up late? Sorry, it has been proven by science that happiness, health and professional success belong more to people who wake up early. Getting up early allows you to make time for all your little morning habits and more time to create an atmosphere of serenity and confidence that makes the rest of the day less stressful.

How to adopt a morning ritual that calms the mind and how to maintain it?

•Estimate how much time you can spend based on how long you sleep and when to go to work.

•Learn about morning habits that help you fight anxiety. Pick one or more activities and give it a try, some are better for you than others.

•Morning habits are more effective when you enjoy them and can easily integrate them into your life.

•It's easier to get into a new habit if you set clear, specific goals rather than making a general statement like "I want to exercise".

•Make some preparations the day before: prepare your sports outfit, leave your diary visible, set reminders ...

•Know that you are not going to follow this routine to the letter every day. Prepare for the motivation drops. This will make you less likely to make you feel guilty when they occur.

•Get up early and work out the specific activities you want to fit into your routine and the order in which you want to do them. By doing things over and over and in the same order, you will eventually develop habits that would become like automatisms, so you don't need to think anymore.

What good habits have you chosen to incorporate into your morning?

> Are you often late? People who are always late are often anxious.

Here are some tips:

•Make a to-do list. Prioritize what's most important on the list.

•Do not overload your schedule with commitments, and be realistic about the time it will take to do each thing.

•The preparation of satchels and outfits is preferably done in the evening before bedtime.

•Plan a specific place for essential items such as glasses, phone, keys.

•Try to sleep earlier in order to be in good shape when you wake up.

•Always plan to arrive 15 minutes early, regardless of the appointment.

•Set alarms on your phone before you have to leave. As soon as they ring, immediately finish whatever you're doing or tell others you need to leave, log off, gather your things, and say goodbye.

•Change your routine so you don't fall back into the habits that put you behind schedule.

•The success of a good organization is gradual. You can't change everything overnight.

What are your tips for not being late?

Check to see if your job is a source of anxiety. Your job is an integral part of your daily life, so make sure that you job is truly part of your happiness and not a source o amplifier of stress.

Some strategies for managing anxiety and stress a work:

•Have confidence in yourself. You are capable, but it can sometime take time.

•Act on what you can control that is in your area. There are thing you cannot control that are beyond you and cause great anxiety.

•Being organized at work to reduce your level of anxiety, you jus need to set your priorities. For efficiency it's best to start wit the most difficult tasks and/or the ones you like the least, and i gives pride and motivation to have completed a more problemati task.

•Manage deconcentration factors such as noise, heat or cold, phon calls, e-mails. Knowing how to filter and manage information flows a good practice for reducing stress at work. Make sure to set u your workspace in an ergonomic and user-friendly way.

•Avoid conflict at work so as not to add stress. It's all about self management, hindsight and peace of mind.

•Taking breaks is essential for your concentration and well-bein Enjoy free time by doing activities that free the mind.

Avoid traffic jams to decrease stress and anxiety. Whether commuting to work, on the way home, or just traveling, traffic is unfortunately part of our routine and spending some time behind the wheel could have serious mental health consequences and even lead to exhaustion.

Some tips to better manage your stress at the wheel:

•If you know the road is long, put on comfortable shoes before entering traffic.

•Pick a lane and stick to it instead of constantly looking for a faster option. You will avoid traffic stress without wasting much time during rush hour.

•Change the air to relax during rush hour by plugging in an aromatherapy diffuser (eg lavender) to diffuse stress-relieving scents in your car.

•Mindfulness reduces stress and anxiety. It is of course difficult to take refuge in a state of deep meditation while driving, but don't let that prevent you from learning the techniques. Feel your every breath and pay attention to everything around you.

•Remember, you are there because you have made life and career choices, so you can feel in control of your life and minimize your anxieties.

•Think of carpooling, public transport. Let yourself be taken to work while taking advantage of the shuttle time to better organize your day, answer your emails, read, write or simply relax.

Write down the techniques you use along the way to reduce anxiety.

At the end of a hard day's work, nothing better than a good hot bath to calm down, relax and rejuvenate. A hot water bath reduces the harmfulness of stress, calms the nervous system, improves blood circulation, stimulates the immune system, improves the quality of sleep and increases the production of the happiness hormones "endorphins". Overall to live in better health.

To take a more relaxing bath:

•You can take a bath whenever you want. But if you are looking to enjoy a ritual to improve your sleep. Bathing in hot water about one to two hours before bed can shorten the time it takes to fall asleep.

•Create a soothing, serene and minimalist atmosphere like lighting candles.

•The choice of temperature is important. Between 93 and 100 degrees Fahrenheit (34 to 38 ° C), a bath is relaxing.

•Add unscented bath salts or Epsom salts to your bath. They are great for soothing muscles.

•Add a few drops of essential oils to pleasantly scent your bath. Lavender is preferred and particularly good for getting back to sleep.

•It is also nice to have something to do during your bath, such as reading a book.

•While bathing, you can do meditation to further deepen your relaxation.

•After a fifteen minutes, you can do a good, vigorous exfoliation.

•A bath is beneficial as long as its duration is proportionate to the needs of the body. If you prolong this pleasure, you risk cooling you down and coming out wrinkled.

•Hot water tends to dehydrate your skin. Make sure you use a good moisturizer.

What is your bathing ritual for getting the most health benefits?

Use aromatherapy for anxiety. Most commonly in the form of essential oils some of which have calming and relaxing properties that can increase the release of neurotransmitters (e.g. serotonin and dopamine), which will help you relax and calm your mind.

The following essential oils can be used for anxiety:

Basil-Bergamot-Chamomile-Clary sage-Geranium-Fennel-Frankincense-Jatamansi-Lavender-Lemon balm-Mandarin-Marjoram-Neroli-Orange-Patchouli-Peppermint-Petitgrain-Rose-Sandalwood-Valerian-Vetiver-Ylang Ylang

Here are different ways to use the oils:

•Essential oils can be used as part of your bath, adding a few drop of the oil of your choice to the water.

•You can use an essential oil diffuser to make your home a haven o relaxation.

•For portable use, put a few drops of the oil on a tissue to keep i your pocket or on an aromatherapy bracelet or necklace.

•It can be used as part of a self-massage. Make sure to dilute th oils first with a carrier oil (like sweet almond oil). Use about fiv drops of essential oil with about 10 ml of carrier oil for concentration of 1.5% to 3.0%. If you apply the oil on your face, th concentration of essential oils should not exceed 1.5%.

•Consult a practitioner, who can target aromatherapy on you problem and also give additional advice. Attention essential oils ca be dangerous in pregnant women, breastfeeding women, childre and people with other diseases.

What essential oils can you use for aromatherapy? How can you use them? What are the effects on you?

You live in messy? Clutter greatly affects the way you feel at home. Clutter causes excessive stimuli, distracts you from other things you want to focus on, and makes it harder to relax mentally and physically, which increases your anxiety.

Minimize clutter at home by:

•Get the whole family involved to make your home a stress free environment.

•Create slots (drawers and cabinets) for items that are used frequently.

•Get rid of things you don't use. If you use them infrequently and want to keep them, consider storing them in a well-labeled box.

•Put things back in place after using them.

•Sort the dirty laundry by placing the soiled clothes directly in the laundry basket. On the other hand, the parts that can still be reused are to be stored in the cupboard.

Is your home a concern? To what degree? Do you get lost in the mess? What is the source of this mess?

Establish rules to declutter your home.

Do you live in an environment where there is noise pollution? Noise nuisance is associated with a higher prevalence of anxiety. Through exposure to stressful noise, the amygdala, an area of the brain that helps process emotions, sends a distress signal to the hypothalamus, in turn immediately signals the adrenal glands to pump adrenaline (stress hormone) in the blood.

Causes of noise pollution:

•Home Sounds, if there is a lot of activity in the house, including a TV that is always on.

•Workplace Noise. Like assembly lines or noisy construction sites, this also applies to offices where more and more people are crammed into tight spaces. Colleagues who are talking, tapping their fingers on the desk, or making annoying noises can cause this.

•Traffic noise is one of the most common sources of noise pollution. Interestingly, low levels of traffic noise can be harmful.

•Aircraft noise pollution has a significant negative impact on the health and well-being of those who live near airports.

Some tips to isolate noise:

•In housing, insulate partitions, ceilings and floors; protect yourself from pipe noise; and reduce ventilation noise.

•Improve the insulation of old windows or replace them to block outside noise by using insulating glazing.

•Install acoustic air inlets that let air in but not noise.

•Lower the volume of your television, telephone and headphones. Avoid places that are too noisy, as you may be tempted to increase the sound significantly.

•Favor electronic devices and low-noise household appliances.

•Design and furnish the workplace for low noise emissions.

Identify the sources of noise pollution and the means to prevent and reduce it.

Do you have a strong tendency to think about the past and forget all the good memories? Quickly get rid of all that negativity that is causing your frustration and can plunge you into suffering.

How to break free from the wounds of the past?

•Forgive others for your own good.

•Stop being a victim by letting others take control of your actions and emotions. Taking control could make you feel a lot better.

•Not paying attention to the judgments of others, which are often only in your imagination.

•If you are visiting the past, visit it for positive reasons as it can help you move forward. You will find that the decision of the past was justified by several reasonable reasons and that the reactions were natural and even negative things are not totally negative but relatively, and within negativity there is more positivity.

•You have to know that life gives us lessons, and we learn all the time.

•The most effective way is to live in the present, because the past does not exist and is not real. The only life is now and without explanations or thoughts that obsess you.

Are you suffering from the past? Make your own plan to get rid of your past wounds.

Are you worried about the future? And you can't help but imagine the catastrophic scenarios that could occur. This type of thinking generates a constant feeling of worry and vulnerability.

Tips to stop being afraid of the future:

•The first step is to become aware of the existence of anticipatory thinking.

•To acknowledge the emotion of fear, which cannot be denied.

•Re-train your brain to function differently. For this, you will train yourself to imagine a new scenario for the future situation that causes you concern, looking at the future in a more confident and positive way.

•Imagine the action in the catastrophic event. In fact, you have to try to find the solution to the envisaged disaster, and you realize that the disaster is not so serious. Usually, this allows you to take control of your anxieties.

•When you have an anticipatory thought that causes anxiety, you tend to focus your mind on that thought, so you can run for hours on end without doing anything really useful. To end this process is to deeply realize that the only moment you have is the present moment. To train you to modify your concentration there are several techniques mindfulness meditation, relaxation ...

•See that everything passes, that everything ends. When the painful event you predicted is no longer in the future but in the past, it is good to notice that it is over and the thought was wrong and the fear was just fear of no consequence.

Write down any future issues that worry you. You will find your own way to put this anxiety aside.

Are you stressed out and having trouble falling asleep due to financial issues? You are not alone because money is the greatest source of stress for most people. To manage your anxiety level, it's important to plan well for your financial future.

Some advice to improve your financial future:

•Learn to plan for the future to deal with the unexpected.

•Having a solid financial plan in place can help you track your income and expenses to see where the money is going each month. This will help you keep your expenses below your income.

•Don't live beyond your means.

•A plan for debt repayment and spending using your budget.

•Having an emergency fund will prevent you from going into debt for unforeseen expenses.

•Retirement savings.

•Have multiple sources of income.

Plan your financial future now.

Do you find yourself in annoying discussions? Avoid confrontations which can lead to anxiety. And try to learn to control your mood in discussions.

To improve your skills during difficult conversations:

•Focus on what the other person means instead of responding t accusations and angry words.

•Don't raise your voice because the level of your voice can make big difference in a heated debate.

•Pay attention to your posture as this can make all the difference i a difficult conversation. Maintain a balanced posture and avoi aggressive body language.

•Focus on one issue during the discussion. Do not bring other issue into the discussion or bring up issues from the past. Discussin several different issues at once will increase your chances of losin your temper.

•Some people like to argue because it gives them a temporar feeling of power. Avoid indulging their needs.

•Deep breathing has the power to calm you down. Try to breath slower and deeper than you normally would. You will be able t consciously choose what to do or say.

•You know yourself and your body better than anyone, so as soon a you get nervous and your thoughts start to boil, go away and after break. You are ready and you can resume the discussion, you wi find that you can handle the problem better.

•After the dispute, try to regain your calm by calm breathing progressive muscle relaxation, meditation ...

Note the skills acquired for a successful discussion and their effect on your mental health.

Make others happy to reduce your anxiety levels. Doing good fills you with happiness and contentment in the same degree that the recipient of the act is happy. And it is by giving free of charge, whether through a smile, a simple help, or extending a helping hand to those who need help.

There are many forms of making the other happy, including:

•Providing assistance to the poor and needy.

•Upholding ties of kinship, visiting relatives, and asking about their conditions and needs.

•Honoring the guest and receiving him with a smiling face and worthy hospitality.

•Work to reconcile opponents and resolve disputes between them.

•Spreading the ideas of tolerance among people.

•Encouraging people to do good deeds that contribute to instilling love among people.

•Inspect people's conditions, ask about them, and help them solve their problems.

•Getting involved in charities.

Social media is now an integral part of our life. This can prevent us from socializing or having conversations, is a source of isolation, dissatisfaction and sadness. If you were spending too much time on social media, maybe it's time to reexamine your online habits and find a healthier balance.

Social media isn't all bad, it's a double-edged sword. In fact, it can have many benefits, including:

•Communicate and stay up to date with family and friends.

•Find new friends and communities.

•Find an outlet for your creativity and personal experiences.

•Find a social connection if you live in a remote area.

•Discover valuable sources of information and learning.

Negative aspects of social media, including:

•Negative posts and news impact your mental health. When you are confronted with negative subjects that awaken in you vigilance in the face of threats, you might be sad and anxious.

•Risk of feeling excluded or inadequate. The images you watch on social media are manipulated, they can make you feel uncomfortable about your appearance or what is going on in your own life, which subsequently gives a negative impact on your self-esteem and self-confidence.

•Friendships weaker than those built in real life, responsible for feelings of isolation and loneliness.

•Excessive use leads to loss of control (you may have to pick up your phone every few minutes to check the news or compulsively respond to each alert). This results in a form of addiction.

•Social media can also negatively influence the quality of sleep especially when you use social media 30 minutes before going to bed. It appears to be related to cognitive and emotional stimulation as well as to the blue light emitted by the screen.

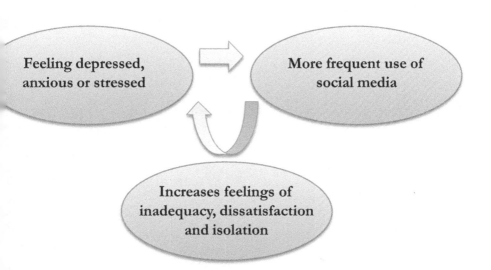

Write actions to change your use of social media to improve mental health.

For example: reduce the time spent online / Use an app to track your time on social media / Turn off social media notifications / Avoid screens at least an hour before going to bed / Change your goal...

Do you spend too much time alone? The body perceives loneliness and social isolation as a form of stress, and its effects on health are as bad as obesity, bad habits such as a sedentary lifestyle, and smoking. People with a tighter social fabric are healthier and less sick than people who live alone or with little social contact.

It's good to have time for oneself, which is necessary for the development of our individuality. But it is essential, for the human being to benefit from it, to alternate between moments of loneliness and times with others.

Some tips for taming loneliness and reaching out to yourself:

•Do activities like reading, playing sports, going for a walk...

•Write experiences, dreams, goals...

•Meditate.

Some tips for breaking isolation and connecting with others:

•Accept your need for connection. You don't have to act like you're perfectly fine without others.

•Volunteer in the community, for example helping people in need.

•Join a group of people who share your interests, such as a book club, a sports team.

•Good discussions can help you fight loneliness.

•Consulting a professional can help you understand the causes and develop an action plan to move forward.

What to do when you are alone?

Avoid keeping your problems to yourself. Pick someone you trust, who may be able to give you some great advice. If you have friends around you, you are more likely to go through life's challenges with greater peace of mind. If necessary, do not hesitate to consult a practitioner who will be able to listen to you and advise you.

Tips can help you to develop and maintain friendship which is often easier said than done:

•Take the first step in finding new friends. It can be simple if you are looking to meet new people, trying to open up to new experiences. If your current hobbies don't involve a lot of socializing, consider a new hobby that offers the opportunity to meet new people.

•Once you've struck up a friendship, you need to make an effort to keep it alive. So keep in touch (call or text every now and then).

•Be the friend you would like to have. Treat your friend the way you want them to treat you.

•Be prepared to listen and support your friends the way you want them to listen and support you.

•Don't set too many rules and expectations. Common ground can help lay the foundation for friendship despite differences.

•Don't be too clingy or needy. Give your friend space, everyone needs space from time to time.

•When there is an obstacle in the path of friendship, try to find a way to overcome the problem. This will often deepen the bond between you.

•Beware, an unhealthy or toxic friendship can cause stress and bring you down just as easily as healthy friendships uplift you.

What is the place of friends in your battle with anxiety? Which friend(s) do you trust to talk about what is stressing you?

Are you not leaving your house? Walking in green spaces often causes a feeling of well-being, calm and peacefulness. Researchers have found that walking in nature is a real therapeutic practice, it significantly reduced anger, anxiety, depression and fatigue.

But why just walking in nature is so effective?

•You are in motion, you relax your mind.

•Acts as a positive regulation of your thoughts.

•Rest your ears and learn to savor the silence.

•Awakening senses.

•During this time it is possible to practice meditation and relaxation.

•**Good for morale**: Reduces stress, anxiety, makes you happier and stimulates your cognitive abilities.

•**Good for the body**: Walking is a physical exercise that burns calories. Walking also stimulates the immune system.

Write down your plans for nature walks. How to benefit more (breathe, meditate ...)?

You need to be able to say no to your family, friends, boss, coworkers. You have to know how to set limits and explain to those around you that you also have to take care of yourself. Sometimes you can say no to some people in some situations, but not in others.

Tips for learning to say "no":

•When you're about to say "no," remember why you're doing it. Focus on the positive things you will get in your life when you refuse (more time with your family, reading, writing, another hobby, or even just relaxing). And so your refusal of things to be able to say yes to the things you want in your life and that there is no time for everything. This positive motivation will help you move forward with your decision, even if it is difficult.

•It becomes easier for people to accept your rejection if you gently refuse. You can do this, for example, by saying that you appreciate the offer, you can add that you don't have the time or the energy for this.

•Some people may be so insistent on overcoming your objections even if you refuse for a good reason. Try telling them how you feel about them not accepting your rejection.

•You can help by suggesting a suitable person to perform the task.

•You may feel a little guilty. Just feel it without acting, it will pass quickly.

•Get people used to your style. Over time, they will become more understanding. It will make life and relationships simpler and more respectful.

What are the things you want to say "no" to? What are the motives? How will you do this?

Also learn to say "yes" to enjoy life. Yes when you have the opportunity to distract yourself from the things that stress you every day. You have to open your mind, be flexible and open your horizons to live beautiful and new adventures, which is good for reducing stress.

Why do you say "yes"?

•Sometimes opportunity comes suddenly and doesn't wait for the perfect timing.

•Opportunities don't always present themselves. Life promotes daring. When making a decision, the "no" answer is often related to regret in one way or another.

•Life is richer, more vibrant. When you say yes, you are doing more, producing more, and living more.

•It attracts positivity. The word "yes" in itself is an invitation and makes you responsible.

•By saying yes, you know what you are capable of and how far you can go.

•Life is short. Don't ask why, but why not?

What are the things you want to say "yes" to? What are the motives?

Do the hobbies you love. It's a good way to free your mind from the things that stress you out. When people engage in leisure activities, they are immediately less stressed and in a better mood. The positive health effects of leisure seem to linger for hours after the activity itself. Be careful, the activity must be mentally engaging to break the cycle of rumination that leads people to immerse themselves in ideas that generate stress. Too many distractions can negate the positive effects.

Some hobbies to try:

- Journaling
- Reading
- Coloring
- Hiking
- Exercise
- Cooking
- Crafts
- Gardening

Try to collect ideas for relaxing hobbies.

Learn how to spend quality time with your family or friends. It is a great way to put aside the stress of everyday life and bring more happiness.

Benefits of spending time with family:

•Reduces stress by relying on friends and family, rather than less desirable ones.

•You create strong emotional support and allow you to externalize repressed emotions which helps you overcome difficulties and reduces the risk of depression.

•Spending time with the family builds the self-confidence of all family members.

•Helps to develop interpersonal communication skills.

•Help parents play their role with their child. Help children to perform well in school and develop social and emotional skills.

To spend quality time with your family:

•Take the time to put the ones you love on your calendar so you can plan to be with them. Your family will feel important to you, and in return, you will be happy to take the time to take care of them.

•Make meals special times for the gathering.

•Make time every day to have fun together. With the little ones play entertaining games.

•When taking time with the family, turn off everything (TV, smartphones, electronics, etc.). A simple hour when you are 100% with your child is much better than a whole day when you are distracted.

•Find activities that everyone enjoys to spend quality time, which is why it is important to listen to all members of the family, and to respect each other's choices and tastes.

•Plan a family vacation.

Your plan for spending quality time with your family.

Are you aware of the positive effects of laughter? Laughter allows you to swallow large amounts of air which is good for the heart and promotes good blood circulation, lowers stress hormones like adrenaline, and strengthens the immune system. Laughter stimulates the body to release feel-good hormones "endorphins" that reduce pain, aid the healing process, and relieve anxiety and stress. Laughter is the fastest way to create a positive state of mind and improve your mood, create and strengthen human bonds, and improve self-confidence. It feels good to laugh!

Ways to bring more laughter into your life:

•Decide to laugh more.

•Add laughter to your morning routine to help prepare you for great day.

•Smile more. When you smile, the changes start to happen automatically. You can think of a smile as the start of a laugh.

•Do more of what makes you laugh, and try to maximize the amount of humor in your life.

•Try Inner Smile Meditation. Sit comfortably. Breathe slowly and deeply for a few seconds. Close your eyes, and think of something that makes you very happy (like a child's smile). Inhale this happiness like a perfume until your chest opens and expands, and as you exhale, let this happiness spread throughout your body. Add smile to your face to amplify the sensation. Your face is relaxed and soothed, it connects you to the best of yourself.

•Laugh with others using humor. This way will probably be easier because laughter is contagious and is a natural social activity.

•Laugh with others without humor. You don't need a funny stimulus to laugh with others. In fact, social laughter is often less about humor than connection.

What's your strategy for adding more laughs to your life?
Write down its impact on your mental health.

Learn to laugh at yourself to increase your self-confidence and reduce your anxiety levels. Making fun of yourself is not making a fool of yourself. But it is knowing how to use humor to play down many situations in life. It is very effective in building sympathy as you intentionally ignore your self-esteem and can lighten the mood and defuse tense or difficult situations. By accepting your weaknesses and flaws, you reveal your strength.

Practical advice for laughing at yourself:

•Accept that you are imperfect.

•Practice self-mockery.

•To be more effective, self-mockery must be accompanied by non-verbal language that reassures your credibility (posture, body language, etc.).

•Self-mockery should be caring and self-loving.

•Be careful not to laugh at yourself too much, so as not to belittle yourself. Also be careful that others do not exceed certain limits.

•Avoid laughing when you are at a disadvantage.

Practice self-deprecation. Watch your ability to laugh at your flaws and mistakes and its impact on your mood.

Optimize to-do lists to calm down and relax. To-do lists can be an important tool in controlling your stress and anxiety levels. When you have mini-goals in front of you which are the steps of a plan, it is much easier to organize your time effectively and put things in perspective, and it will help to set aside the goal that generates the anxiety and focus on other things. Crossing off completed tasks one after another has very beneficial effects on stress levels.

Tips for making an effective to-do list:

•Break down the tasks on your list into easier-to-plan tasks and balance the workload they represent.

•An effective to-do list should not be overloaded. It is better to write down the main, most important and/or most urgent actions rather than making an exhaustive list of tasks that will quickly discourage you.

•For each day, at most one priority task, several secondary tasks and small tasks of low importance.

•Estimate the time you will devote to a task and the effort. This helps prioritize tasks. Do not forget to set aside between 10% and 20% of your day to deal with the unforeseen, which also gives more chance for planned tasks to be carried out.

•Create a visual and pleasant to do list. Colors are for example a good way to quickly identify the important or urgent task.

Note the tools used to create to-do lists, your discipline
and its impact on quality of life.

An up-to-date agenda will allow you to decrease your stress and fight anxiety. It will allow you to free your mind from all the tasks to be memorized by putting them on paper. Your agenda could become your best companion.

To take advantage of your diary:

•Your diary is your tool to put on paper all the ideas that run through your head to get them out of your mind, it allows you to get rid of ideas that generate anxiety.

•Writing down your emotions helps to accept and assimilate them and will definitely help clean up your head.

•It is recommended to put everything in your diary: appointment; travel time; time at work ...

•Try to reduce unforeseen events as much as possible by regularly planning your agenda.

•Leisurely prepare for the event by planning a few days in advance and noting the steps for a successful showdown.

•Every morning, view the diary in order to plan the day.

•When the agenda is full, learn to say "no" to limit sources of stress.

•Pair your calendar with your to-do list. These 2 tools will allow you to effectively manage your time and stay zen.

How can the agenda help you fight anxiety? Choose the model that suits you for efficient use.

Made in the USA
Monee, IL
05 July 2022

99124965R00066